King Arthur
and the Knights
of the Round Table

Simplified by Michael West

Revised by D K Swan

Longman

<u>1200 word</u>
<u>vocabulary</u>

Longman Group Limited
London

Associated companies, branches and representatives throughout the world

© Longman Group Ltd 1955 and 1976

First published 1955
New impressions 1965; 1966; 1967; 1968 (twice);
1969; 1970; 1971; 1972
Second edition 1976
New impression 1979

ISBN 0 582 53415 1

Note
Words with a star ★ are outside Stage 1 of the New Method Supplementary Readers. These extra words are in a list on page 60

Acknowledgement
We are grateful to the British Film Institute for supplying the following photographs, & also to the following film companies for permission to reproduce copyright photographs: Metro Goldwyn Mayer Inc., for 'Knights of the Round Table' © 1954; Loew's Inc. for p. iv, 33, 56; ColumbiaWarner Film Distributors for 'Camelot' p. 17, 23; Universal City Studios Inc., for 'War Lord' p. 37. Cover photograph supplied by the Kobal Collection.We thank Metro Goldwyn Mayer for their permission to use this picture.

Printed in Hong Kong by Yu Luen Offset Printing Factory Limited
Set in 14/15½ Bembo

Contents

Chapter 1
Arthur and Merlin

This is the story of a great King who lived in Britain. It is a very old story. Men have added magic to it. But there WAS a King Arthur. No one knows just where in Britain he lived, or when he lived, but he was a person—not just a fairy story.

King Uther and Igraine have a son

Once there was a King in Britain called King Uther. He was a great and good king. He loved the beautiful Princess Igraine, and he wanted to marry her, but she did not love him. He was very sad, and everyone thought that he would die.

There was a magician named Merlin. He could change himself into any animal or bird; he could change so that no one could see him. He could go from place to place by magic. One day Merlin came to King Uther. He said, 'King Uther, I will help you. You shall marry Princess

Igraine, and she will have a son. I will help you if you will give that son to me.'

'I will give him to you,' said the King.

Uther gives his son to Merlin, and then dies

So King Uther married Igraine, and they had a son. They named the son, Arthur. When Arthur was three days old, a very old man was seen at the door of the King's House. It was Merlin.

Then King Uther took the child in his arms and went out and gave him to Merlin.

Soon after that, King Uther became very ill. He knew that he was going to die. Then Merlin said, 'Call all your knights and great men and tell them, "My son, Arthur, will be king after me!"'

King Uther did that before he died. But all the knights and great men began to fight: each wanted to make himself king. Merlin took Arthur away. He gave the child to a good knight named Sir Ector. Arthur grew up with Sir Ector's son, Kay, and became a man.

The Sword in the Stone

When Arthur was a man, Merlin went to the Archbishop★ (the head of the Church) and said, 'Call all the great men of Britain to London.

Then they shall see the man who will be their King.'

All the great men came to London. They went into the church, and the Archbishop spoke to them. When they came out of the church they saw in front of the church door a great stone. There was a sword in the stone, and there was writing on the stone:

THE MAN WHO CAN TAKE THIS SWORD OUT OF THE STONE IS THE KING OF BRITAIN

All the knights tried, one after another, to take the sword out of the stone; but none of them could do it. The sword would not come out.

Arthur becomes King

At the same time there was a great joust⋆ in London. All the great knights jousted in it. They began on their horses with spears. They rode quickly, and met—CRASH! Some knights fell off their horses, and then they fought on foot with swords.

Sir Ector went to the joust with Sir Kay and Arthur. The two young men wanted to joust, but Sir Kay had no sword.

Arthur said, 'There is a sword in a stone outside a church. I saw it on the way here. I'll get it and fight with it, and you can have my sword, Sir Kay.'

They rode to the church. Arthur got off his horse; he took the sword in his hand—and it came out of the stone.

They went back to the field. When Sir Ector saw the sword, he kissed Arthur's hand and said, 'You are my King.'

They went to the Archbishop. Then the Archbishop called all the knights.

The Archbishop said, 'Put the sword back into the stone.' Arthur put the sword back into the stone. All the knights tried again to take it out, but it did not move.

Arthur took it out again. So they cried out, 'Arthur is King! Arthur is King!'

They all went into the church, and the Archbishop made Arthur King of Britain.

The Round Table

So Arthur became King. He married the most beautiful lady in England, Princess Guinevere, and she became his Queen.

Then Merlin made the Round Table.

There were 150 places at the table. Each knight had his name written in his place. There were 128 knights at the table. As time went on other brave and good knights came, and King

Arthur gave them places. One place was not filled for a long time. That place was for a knight who had never done any bad thing to anyone. It was called the 'Seat Perilous': if a bad man sat in it, he would die. After many years Sir Galahad came and was given that place.

Chapter 2
The Sword, Excalibur

King Arthur comes to the Castle of Queen Annoure

King Arthur went all over the country, getting to know his people and helping them. After many days he came to a great forest. He was still in the forest when evening came. Then he saw in front of him a castle. It was the biggest and most beautiful castle he had ever seen.

As he came nearer, the great door of the castle opened and a lady came out.

She said, 'King Arthur, I ask you to stay in my castle. Night is near, and you must have food and a bed.'

'I thank you,' said King Arthur, and he went in.

After they had eaten, Queen Annoure told one of her men to lead the King to his bedroom.

Queen Annoure wants the King to stay in her castle

Next morning Queen Annoure said, 'I'll show you my castle and all the beautiful things that I have in it. I have more jewels and gold and riches than any living person.'

They went from room to room, and each room was richer and more beautiful than the last: Queen Annoure was a magician. Then they came out on to the top of the castle. The Queen said, 'See those beautiful gardens and all those green fields. They are all mine. And see that great wall on all sides. Stay here with me and be king of all this. You can't get away: the door of the castle is shut, and that great wall is on all sides. And my men stand ready to make you stay or to kill you if I tell them to do so.'

King Arthur said, 'I think nothing of your magic. Your servants can't kill me and they can't make me stay.'

Then, with his sword in hand, Arthur went out of the castle, and out through the door in the great wall. Nobody could stop him.

King Arthur fights Sir Pellinore

The house of Sir Pellinore was not far from the castle of Queen Annoure. Queen Annoure sent a man to him, saying, 'A very bad knight is coming to my castle. He wants to kill me and take my jewels and my gold. He is on his way near your house. Go out and fight him, and save me.'

So Sir Pellinore came out against King Arthur. He rode against the King with his spear, and Arthur was thrown from his horse. Then they fought with swords. They fought on—and on. Then the King's sword broke★.

'Ha!' cried Sir Pellinore, 'you have lost the fight.'

Arthur threw down his broken sword; then he ran at Sir Pellinore, and took him in his arms; he threw him down on the grass and set his foot on his head.

Arthur took off his helmet★. Sir Pellinore looked up and saw his face. 'It's the King!' he cried. 'I didn't know.' He told Arthur what Annoure had said; and they were friends.

King Arthur finds the sword, Excalibur

King Arthur had broken his sword in the fight against Sir Pellinore. Merlin came to him and said, 'Come with me, and you shall get the best sword that was ever made. It's a magic sword.'

The King went with Merlin through the forest. The trees shut out the daylight, and Arthur could not see the sky. After a long time they came to an open place where there were no trees, but a lake★ of water. As Arthur stood by the lake he saw an arm with a sword in its hand come up out of the water.

'Go and take it,' said Merlin. 'It is the sword Excalibur. It was made for you by the Lady of the Lake, who lives in her home in the water of the lake.'

There was a boat at the side of the lake. King Arthur got into the boat and went and took the sword. The scabbard★ of the sword was covered with jewels.

'That is a magic scabbard,' said Merlin. 'No man can kill the man who has it.'

Queen Morgan le Fay wants to steal Excalibur

There was a queen named Morgan le Fay. King Arthur did not know that she was a magician and an evil★ woman. He thought that she was good, not evil, and that she was his friend.

One day he went out riding in the forest. He took his spear, but he did not want to take his sword. He gave Excalibur to Queen Morgan le Fay, saying, 'I will come and get it on my way back.'

Arthur rode on in front of the men who were with him. He lost his way in the forest. When night came, he was alone. He saw a little light and rode to it. Then he saw that the light was in a beautiful ship on a lake. The ship was near the side of the lake, so he went on to the ship, and he saw food and drink on the table and a bed, all ready.

'I'll stay here tonight,' he said. 'In the morning I'll find my way back, and get Excalibur, and go home.'

King Arthur in the castle of Sir Damas

So King Arthur ate, and slept. But, when he woke, he saw that he was not in the ship. He was in a little room with a very small window. The door was shut: he could not get out. There were three other men in the room. They were knights.

They said, 'This is the castle of Sir Damas. He is a very evil knight. He caught us and put us here, saying, "You may go out if you will fight for me. If you will not fight for me, you will stay and die here."'

Men came and led Arthur into a great hall in which Sir Damas was sitting.

'Will you fight for me?' Sir Damas asked.

King Arthur said, 'I'll joust for you if you will give me those three knights. Give me those three knights, and, after I have fought for you, we shall all go back to our homes.'

'Yes,' answered Sir Damas. 'You can have the

three knights if you will fight for me.'

Then a man came into the hall and said, 'Queen Morgan le Fay sends King Arthur his sword, Excalibur.'

King Arthur was very glad to have his sword. He made ready to joust.

King Arthur fights Sir Accolon

When Arthur came out to the jousting field he saw another knight waiting there. There was no mark on his shield showing who he was, and his face was hidden so that Arthur could not see it.

The fight began. King Arthur was unhappy: his sword Excalibur did not bite on the other knight's shield. Then he knew that this sword was not Excalibur; it was some other sword made to look like Excalibur.

He fought on. Then Arthur's sword broke.

The other knight said, 'Say that you have lost the fight, and I will not kill you.'

'No!' cried Arthur. 'I will fight on—and on.'

King Arthur takes Excalibur from the knight

Then Arthur hit the knight on the head with his broken sword—so hard that he fell down and his sword fell from his hand. Arthur quickly took the other knight's sword. It was

Excalibur!

The knight had at his side the scabbard.

Arthur took the scabbard; then he said, 'Tell me who you are. What is your name?'

The knight answered, 'I am Sir Accolon, Knight of the Round Table.'

'Why have you fought against me, your King?'

He answered, 'I didn't know that you were King Arthur. I thought that you were Sir Damas. Queen Morgan le Fay said to me, "King Arthur is in the castle of Sir Damas. You must go and fight Sir Damas and save your King." And she said, "Here is King Arthur's sword, Excalibur, and its scabbard. Take them for the fight so that you may save your King."'

King Arthur comes against Sir Damas

King Arthur rode with Sir Accolon and the three knights against Sir Damas. There was a great fight, which King Arthur won.

Sir Damas was brought before the King.

'Why did you do this thing?' said King Arthur.

'Queen Morgan le Fay told me to do it,' answered Sir Damas.

Then the King said, 'You are no knight. You shall not have a sword or shield. I take from you your castle and all that you have and give them to your younger brother.'

Morgan le Fay was at Camelot while Arthur was away. She heard that King Arthur was alive. She went to Queen Guinevere and said, 'I must go back to my own country. My people want me to go back to them.'

Queen Guinevere answered, 'Don't go. The King will soon be here. He will be glad to see you.' (Queen Guinevere did not know what Morgan le Fay had done!)

'No! No!' said Morgan le Fay. 'I must go. I must go now.' And she rode away alone on her black horse.

Morgan le Fay steals the scabbard

Morgan le Fay rode her black horse all that day, and all the night. She asked all the people she saw, 'Where is King Arthur? Tell me, where is the King?'

At last she saw a man who said, 'The King is ill. He had a hard fight at the castle of Sir Damas, and he is now in the House of the Good Women.'

The good women worked for God and gave help to people who were ill or poor.

Morgan le Fay rode on and came to the House of the Good Women. She said, 'I have come from far away. I have been riding day and night; please give me food.'

They brought food to her.

'Is there any other person here, in this house?' she asked.

They said, 'Yes. King Arthur is here. He is sleeping.'

'Oh! The King!' she cried. 'I cannot stay to speak with him: I must go on. But may I look at him? May I see his face? I love him so much! I will not wake him.'

The good women said, 'Yes; you may go and look at him; but don't make a noise. Don't wake him.'

Morgan le Fay went into the King's room. She stood at his side as he slept. She saw that the King had his hand on the sword, Excalibur: she could not take it away without waking him. Then she saw the scabbard at the foot of the bed. She took it and hid it in her clothes and went out of the room, and got on her black horse and rode quickly away.

The King rides after Morgan le Fay

The King opened his eyes; he saw that the scabbard had gone. He called the good women and said, 'Did anyone come into this room when I was sleeping?'

14

They said, 'Queen Morgan le Fay came—
but no other person. She could not stay to speak
with you, but she wanted to look at your face
because she loves you so much.'

'I thank you,' said the King. 'Thank you for
having me here in your house. You have been
very good to me. . . . I must go now. I must go
after Queen Morgan le Fay. She has taken the
scabbard of Excalibur.'

He was still not well, but they could not
make him stay. So the good women helped him
to get on his horse, and he rode away.

He rode on, and on. At last he came to a
river. There was a man there with his cows in a
field. The King asked, 'Has anyone come this
way?'

'Yes,' answered the man. 'A beautiful lady
came on a black horse. She went across the river
here, and she rode on, very quickly.'

King Arthur went over the river and through
a forest, and up a hill. Then he looked down,
and he saw Morgan le Fay far away.

The scabbard is lost and never seen again

Morgan le Fay looked back and she saw the
King. She rode on, over a place covered with
stones, then down a hill to a lake. The water in
the lake was black. No animal drank it. No

birds sang in the trees.

She got off her black horse and took the scabbard and threw it far away into the water.

'King Arthur shall never have it!' she cried. 'That scabbard shall not save him from all who fight against him. No one will ever find it there!'

Then she rode away.

King Arthur came to the place. He could not see Morgan le Fay or know which way she had gone. He could not see the marks of her horse's feet because of the stones.

So Morgan le Fay went back to her own country and stayed there.

King Arthur had the sword Excalibur; but the scabbard was never found.

Chapter 3
Vivien and Merlin

Merlin knows that his time has come

When King Arthur was young, Merlin the Magician helped him in every way. He showed him how to be a good king and a brave knight. He helped him to rule well, so that all the people loved him. He helped him to build the beautiful city, Camelot. But Merlin became old, and he knew that Arthur must help himself and do without the help of magic. He said to Arthur, 'I shall not be with you much longer. I shall go down alive into a cave, and I shall not be able to come up out of it to help you.'

Arthur said, 'Can't you save yourself by your magic?'

'No,' answered Merlin. 'I can't. What must be, will be.'

Vivien comes to Camelot

The Lady Vivien came to Camelot. She had lived with the Lady of the Lake (who made Excalibur). The Lady of the Lake was a great magician, and Vivien knew all her magic. When Vivien knew all the Lady of the Lake's magic, she went to Camelot and worked with Merlin. When she knew all Merlin's magic she thought, 'Now I know more magic than Merlin. He is an old man; I can't kill him, but I can shut him up somewhere. Then I shall be the greatest of all magicians.'

The Magic Cave

Vivien went with Merlin to a far country where there was a great hill of stone. In it there was a magic cave.

Merlin told Vivien, 'The mouth of the cave is open now, but if you speak magic words they can make it shut.'

'What are the words that will make it open again?' asked Vivien.

'I don't know,' said Merlin. 'I know how to make the door of the cave shut, but I don't know how to open it again.'

'I want to go into the cave,' she said. 'Come in with me.'

So Merlin went into the cave; but Vivien ran quickly out, and said the magic words. The mouth of the cave shut, and Merlin could not get out.

Some men say that he is still there. One day, they say, somebody will break open the cave and he will come out and help us all with his magic to be good and happy.

So Arthur had no more help from Merlin.

Chapter 4
Sir Tristram

Tristram's mother dies in the forest

One day the King of Lyonesse was lost in the forest. The Queen was soon going to have a child. When the King did not come back from his riding, she ran out into the forest to find him. She went a long way, and at last she fell at the foot of a tree: there she had her little son. She knew that she was going to die; so she kissed the child and said, 'Ah, little son, your coming has been sad; so your name shall be Tristram, but you will grow up to be a brave and good knight.' ('Tristram' means 'sad one'.)

The King's men found the Queen and the child in the forest and took them back to the castle.

For many days the King did not speak or eat, and men said, 'He will die too, and the little child will be our king.' But at last the King began to live again.

The new Queen wants to kill Tristram

After seven years the King married another queen. The new Queen had a son. She loved her own son very much, but she did not want Tristram. She wanted to kill him.

The Queen got some poison★ and put it ready for Tristram to drink when he came back from riding.

'He'll die when he drinks it,' she thought.

But the Queen's son came in before Tristram and drank the poison, and died.

Again she got poison and set it ready for Tristram, but the King came into the room. He put his hand out to take the poison, but she cried out, 'Don't drink it!'

Then the King remembered how her son had died, and he knew what she wanted to do. He said, 'You wanted to poison Tristram, but your son drank the poison. So again you set poison for Tristram, but I was going to drink it.'

Then he told his servants to take the Queen and make a great fire and burn her.

The fire was made ready. Then Tristram threw himself down at his father's feet and said, 'Father, do not do this thing! Take her back, and love her, and she will love you and be a good Queen; but send me away.'

Tristram goes to King Mark

Then Tristram went and lived with his father's brother, Mark. Mark was King of Cornwall. Tristram grew up and became a very brave and strong★ man.

Sir Marhaus was the son of the King of Ireland; he was very brave and strong. He was the strongest of all knights. No one could stand against him in a fight. He came in his ship to the castle of King Mark and he said, 'Say that you will be my man and do all that I tell you to do, or send one of your knights to fight me.'

Not one of King Mark's knights would go to fight Sir Marhaus. They knew that he was too strong. Then Tristram said, 'I am not a boy now: I am a man. Make me a knight and send me.'

At last King Mark said, 'I do not want to send you, but I have no other man to send.'

Tristram fights Sir Marhaus

So Sir Tristram and Sir Marhaus fought. They fought all day. Sir Marhaus was strong, but he was older than Sir Tristram, and he was not so quick on his feet. Tristram was younger and very quick; Sir Marhaus could not hit him. The sun was hot, and, as the day went on, Sir Marhaus did not fight so strongly. Then at last Tristram's sword cut through Sir Marhaus's helmet and wounded* him in his head so that he died, and his men took him away to his ship.

Sir Tristram's wound will not heal

Sir Tristram was wounded too. It was a very bad wound. There was poison in it and it stayed open and did not heal*.

No one could make Sir Tristram's wound begin to heal. At last an old woman came and said, 'The poison in the wound came from

Ireland. You must send Sir Tristram to Ireland.
There someone will make it heal.'

Sir Tristram goes to Ireland

So King Mark sent Sir Tristram in a ship to
Ireland, but Sir Tristram called himself by
another name, because he had killed Sir
Marhaus, son of the King of Ireland.

Tristram played the harp★ very beautifully.
The King of Ireland heard him playing as his
ship came near, and he brought him to his
castle. He told the Princess Isolt to heal
Tristram's wound.

So Isolt made Tristram's wound heal, and
Tristram showed her how to play the harp.
They were very happy, like brother and sister.

Tristram fights Sir Palamides

There was a knight named Sir Palamides. He
loved Isolt and asked her again and again to
marry him. She did not like him, and she told
him to go away, but he would not go. He made
her very unhappy. There was a joust and Sir
Palamides came to it. He had black armour and
a black shield, and he rode a black horse. Tristram got white armour and a white shield, and
he rode a white horse. He rode at Sir Palamides
with his spear, so that the black knight fell over

the back of his horse. Then Tristram stood over him with his sword and said, 'Go away from here and don't speak to Isolt again—or I will kill you!'

King Mark marries Isolt

Sir Tristram went back to Cornwall. He told King Mark about Isolt and how good she was. Then King Mark said, 'I have no wife. If I marry Isolt, the King of Ireland and I will be friends, and there will be no more fighting. It will be good for my people if I marry Isolt. Go and ask the King of Ireland to give me Isolt to be my Queen.'

So Tristram went to Ireland. The King of Ireland said, 'Yes; it will be a good thing for this country and for Cornwall.' And he sent Isolt to King Mark.

Tristram took Isolt on his ship to go to Cornwall. The ship came to Cornwall and he said sadly, 'I am going away to Camelot to become a Knight of the Round Table and fight for King Arthur; but if ever you want my help, I will come.'

Sir Palamides takes Isolt away on his horse

One day when Isolt was walking in the forest,

Sir Palamides came and took her up and put her on his horse and rode away. Another knight rode after him. Sir Palamides heard the knight coming, and he got off his horse to fight. Then Isolt ran away. She went on and on through the forest. Night was coming on, and there was no help. Then she saw a lake, and she said, 'I'll throw myself into the water and die; then I shall be saved from Sir Palamides.'

Sir Atherp takes Isolt to his castle

Just as Isolt was going to throw herself into the lake she heard someone coming. It was a knight named Sir Atherp. Sir Atherp saw Isolt standing there, and he said, 'Can I help you? Why are you alone in the forest, with night coming on?'

She answered, 'I ran away from Sir Palamides. He'll come through the forest and catch me and take me away. O save me from him!'

Sir Atherp said, 'Come with me into my castle. I'll save you from Sir Palamides.'

So Sir Atherp led Isolt to his castle.

Soon Sir Palamides came riding through the forest and came to the door of the castle. The door was shut. He cried, 'Open the door!' but no one answered.

Tristram comes to save Isolt

Sir Tristram was riding on his way to Camelot. A man ran and told him, 'Sir Palamides has taken Isolt away on his horse.' Then Tristram came quickly back. He found a knight wounded in the forest and took him to a hut. It was the knight who had fought Sir Palamides.

'Where did Isolt go?' Sir Tristram asked the wounded man.

'I don't know where she went,' answered the knight. 'She ran away when she saw us fighting.'

Sir Tristram went on and saw a lake. He saw the marks of feet near the water, and the marks of a horse. He went on and came to a castle. The door of the castle was shut, and outside the door of the castle he saw Sir Palamides.

Sir Palamides saw Tristram and rode at him. But Sir Tristram's spear sent Palamides back over his horse on to the grass. Sir Palamides stood up and took his sword. Then Tristram got off his horse and took his sword; and they fought with swords there in front of the castle. Isolt looked down from a window and saw that Tristram had come to save her. She saw Palamides fall and she saw Tristram stand over him, and she cried out, 'Don't kill him!'

Sir Atherp's men opened the door of the

castle and she ran out. She said, 'Don't kill him, Sir Tristram. He fights bravely. Send him to King Arthur and he will become a good knight and fight for others, not for himself.'

So Sir Palamides went to Camelot, to King Arthur, and he became a very good knight, and all men said good things about him.

Tristram comes to Cornwall

Sir Tristram brought Isolt back to King Mark, and he stayed in Cornwall for some time.

Now King Mark began to be afraid of Sir Tristram. He thought, 'Sir Tristram is young and brave. He fought twice against Sir Palamides and saved my Queen Isolt from him. Now she will love him, and will not love me.'

One day Tristram was sitting with Isolt near the sea. He was playing on his harp, and Isolt was happy hearing it. Then King Mark came out at him with a sword and killed him, and he fell dead at the feet of Isolt.

Day after day, Isolt sat looking out over the sea. She would not eat or drink or speak. And so she died too.

King Arthur heard what King Mark had done, and he sent a knight, who came to Cornwall and killed him.

Chapter 5
Gareth and Linet

Gareth comes to King Arthur

One day King Arthur was sitting with Queen Guinevere and all his knights at the Round Table, and a big, strong young man came into the hall.

'Who are you, and what do you want?' asked King Arthur.

'My name is Gareth. I have come to ask you for three things,' he said. 'I'll ask one of them now. I ask that I may eat and drink here every day for one year.'

The King said, 'Yes: you may do that. You'll be with Sir Kay and do what he says.'

You remember from Chapter 1 that King Arthur grew up to be a man with Sir Kay in the house of Sir Kay's father. Sir Kay was now a Knight of the Round Table. Sir Kay looked at the young man and said, 'That man is not a knight. If he was a knight or the son of a knight, he would ask for a horse and armour. He is some farm boy. He shall have food and work with my men.'

Sir Lancelot was the bravest and strongest of all King Arthur's knights. He said, 'He looks strong, but he's young. He didn't ask for a horse and armour because he's very young now; but he'll grow up and he may be stronger than any of us. He may eat with us.'

'No,' answered the young man; 'I must do what Sir Kay says. I'll work and eat with his men.'

Linet comes to ask King Arthur's help

After one year the young man, Gareth, came again into the great hall where King Arthur sat with his knights. There was a beautiful lady standing in front of the King. She said, 'O King, my name is Linet. I have come to ask your help. My sister has been taken away by four knights to their castle. They call themselves Morning, Noon, Evening and Night. Send one of your knights to save her. Send Sir Lancelot.'

Gareth cried out, 'O King, may I go?'

'Yes, Gareth,' said King Arthur, 'you may go.'

The Lady Linet looked at Gareth: she thought that he was one of the knights' men. 'I asked for Sir Lancelot,' she said, 'and you have sent me this cook's boy.'

Gareth and Linet set out and meet Morning

The King gave Gareth armour, and he rode
away with Linet. She rode in front and she
would not speak to him.

They came to a river. On the far side of it
there was a red tent, and in front of the tent
there was a man in blue armour. This was the
knight who called himself 'Morning'.

'Do you want to run away, cook's boy?' said
Lady Linet. 'Run before he comes at you and
kills you.'

Gareth did not answer, but he went over the
river. They fought on their horses with spears.
Then they took their swords. Gareth's shield
was cut away from his arm, but he fought on.
At last Morning lay on the grass at his feet.

'Don't kill me!' he cried.

'If the Lady Linet asks me, you may live.
What do you ask me to do?'

Linet answered, 'I ask you nothing, cook's
boy.'

'Then I'll kill him!'

'Then—I ask you. Don't kill him.'

Gareth fights Noon

They rode on. Linet rode in front—but not so
far in front, because she had seen how bravely
Gareth fought with Morning.

The sun was hot. They came at last to a river, and there Gareth saw Noon.

'Who are you?' cried Noon.

'This,' said Lady Linet, 'is a cook's boy. King Arthur has sent him to fight you. He has fought your brother, and now he has come against you.'

Noon rode his horse into the river, and they fought there with swords, in the water.

Gareth wounded Noon with his sword four times, and he fell from his horse into the water.

'Your sword did not throw him down,' said Linet: 'his horse fell.'

Gareth did not answer. He took Noon's shield, and they rode on.

Gareth fights Evening

It was now afternoon. They came to a hill, and from the top of the hill Gareth looked down on a great river.

They rode down the hill. Then Gareth saw a man standing by the river. His armour was red, and on his shield there was a red evening sun. He saw the golden sun on Gareth's shield and called out, 'Ho! Noon! Why have you come here?'

'This is not your brother,' said Linet. 'This is a boy whom King Arthur has sent. He has fought your two brothers, and now he has come against you.'

Evening rode at Gareth, but Gareth's spear caught him and threw him from his horse.

They fought with swords. Gareth thought, 'I have fought two knights today, but this man hasn't fought before: he's strong. I can't go on! I can't win!'

Then Linet began to cry out, 'Fight on, Gareth! Fight on! Hit harder!'

Evening came at Gareth. He tried to hit Gareth's head. But the sword hit Gareth's sword, and Evening's sword broke in his hand. Then Gareth took Evening in his arms and threw him down into the river.

He came back to Linet. 'Lead on,' he said, 'and show me the fourth and last knight.'

'No,' answered Linet. 'You have fought bravely: now you shall ride at my side.... Men say that Night is the bravest and strongest of the four. He is as strong as ten men. We will stay here and eat before you come to him.'

They ride on and come to the castle

They rode on, up a hill and came to a cave. There Linet made a fire, and they ate and drank as the sun went down and night came on. Then they rode on.

Linet said at last, 'That is the place.'

Gareth saw a castle standing up against the sky. In front of the door of the castle there was a black tent.

Gareth called, 'Ho, there! Come out!'

A light was seen in the tent, and lights came into the windows of the castle.

'Ho, there!' cried Gareth again.

Then out from the tent there came a knight in black armour, riding on a black horse. On his shield was the picture of a dead man's head. Linet was afraid: she shut her eyes.

Gareth looked at the black knight and said, 'If you are as strong as ten men, why do you want to make me afraid by black armour and that head on your shield? I am not afraid of you. Come on, and fight!'

There was no answer.

Gareth brings Linet and her sister to Camelot

Gareth rode at the knight. Linet heard the crash of Gareth's spear against the black armour. She opened her eyes and saw him standing over the black knight. Gareth opened the black knight's helmet, and there he saw the face of a young boy!

'O Knight,' cried the boy, 'do not kill me! My brothers made me do it. They wanted to make men afraid to come to the castle.'

Gareth helped him to stand up, and then they went into the castle, and Linet found her sister. Gareth brought the two sisters to Camelot.

Then Gareth asked the third thing of King Arthur, and Arthur gladly gave it to him: he made Gareth a Knight of the Round Table.

Chapter 6
Geraint and Enid

King Arthur goes riding in the forest

One evening, King Arthur said, 'As soon as the sun is up, I shall go riding in the forest, and all my knights will come with me.'

'I'll come too,' said Queen Guinevere.

But the Queen did not wake. When she was ready to set out there were only two horses; all the other horses had gone with the King. So she rode away with one of her women.

As the Queen rode on she heard someone coming. She looked back and saw one of the Knights of the Round Table named Geraint. He had no armour, because he was dressed for riding in the forest, but he had a sword at his side.

'Why haven't you gone riding with King Arthur?' asked the Queen.

'I didn't hear him set out,' answered Geraint. 'I slept too long.'

'We'll ride on and come to the road through the forest,' said the Queen. 'If we wait there we'll see them.'

Guinevere and Geraint see an Unknown Knight

So Queen Guinevere and Geraint rode on and came to the forest, and sat on their horses waiting to see the King. As they sat there they heard horses, and they saw a dwarf* riding on a little horse, and a lady riding on a white horse, and a knight in armour riding on the biggest horse the Queen had ever seen.

'Tell me, Geraint,' said the Queen, 'what is the name of that knight? Is he one of the Knights of the Round Table?'

'I don't know who he is,' answered Geraint. 'I can't see his face because of his helmet.'

Then the Queen said to her woman. 'Go and ask the dwarf the name of his knight.'

The woman rode up to the dwarf and questioned him, but the dwarf hit her on her face, and she came back to the Queen.

'He wouldn't tell me,' she said; 'and, when I asked him again, he hit me on the face.'

'Did he do that?' cried Geraint. 'Then *I* will go and ask the knight's name!'

So Geraint went. 'Now, dwarf!' he said. 'Tell me the name of your knight!'

'I will not tell you,' said the dwarf. 'He is a great knight, and doesn't want to know you, or your name.'

'I have spoken to greater men than he,' answered Geraint. 'But, if you will not tell me, I will go and ask him myself.'

Then the dwarf hit Geraint on the face. Geraint put his hand to his sword; then he thought, 'No! If I kill the dwarf the knight will come at me. He has armour, but I haven't. I'll go after him. Wherever he goes, I will go, and at last we shall come to some place where I can find armour and fight him.'

Geraint told this to the Queen. She said, 'Go, Geraint, and then come and tell me.'

Geraint rides after the Unknown Knight

So Geraint rode after the Unknown Knight— through fields and through forests, over hills and across rivers and came at last to a city with a castle on a hill.

In the street of the city, men were washing armour, putting shoes on horses, making all ready for a joust. Geraint rode on and up the hill to the castle. It was a beautiful castle, but stones had fallen from the walls, and the road to it was covered with grass. The door was broken and old.

Geraint goes into the Castle of the Old Knight

Geraint called, and after a long time the door was opened by an old man. He was not a door-man: his clothes were the clothes of a knight or a prince, but they were old, and there were holes which had been covered over by bits of other cloth.

'Do you want to speak with me?' asked the old man; 'or is there anything that I can give you?'

'May I stay here for the night?' said Geraint, 'and can you give me some armour so that I may fight in the joust in your city?'

'Come in,' said the old man, 'and I will do what I can.'

He led Geraint into the hall of the castle. There Geraint saw an old lady and a girl. They were poorly dressed.

Geraint sees Enid and loves her

'I have brought someone to stay here for the night', said the old knight. 'Take his horse, Enid, and then go into the city and buy food.'

The girl stood up, and Geraint saw how beautiful she was. She led away the horse, and then went down into the city. Soon she came back bringing food, and she and her mother cooked it. Then they sat down to eat.

The Old Knight loses all that he has

'Tell me,' said Geraint when they had eaten, 'is this your castle, or is it the castle of some other knight?'

'It is my castle,' the old knight answered, 'and at one time all those houses in the city were mine. When my brother died, many years back, his little son lived here with me. When he grew up to be a man, he fought against me and took from me all that I had. So now I live here in this castle, a poor man.'

'Tell me about the knight who rode into the city before me. He had a dwarf and a lady with him. Who is he?' asked Geraint.

'His name is Sir Edyrn. He is a friend of my brother's son,' said the old knight. 'He has come here for the jousting. The bravest knight wins a Golden Bird. He has won it for two years. If he wins it this year, it will become his own.'

Geraint goes out to fight for Enid

'I shall go to the joust,' said Geraint, 'and fight

this knight whose dwarf hit my Queen's woman and would not tell his name.'

Then he told the old man about the knight and the dwarf on the forest road.

'I'll gladly give you armour,' said the old knight, 'but whoever fights in this joust must fight for the lady whom he loves most of all. I can give you armour, my son, but where can you find a lady?'

Then Geraint said, 'If I may do so, I'll fight for your beautiful daughter, and I'll make her my wife and love her as long as I live.'

The old knight and Enid, his daughter, were very happy to hear Geraint say this.

As soon as the sun was up, the old knight came to Geraint carrying some beautiful but very old armour. Then they went to the jousting field. There were very many people there.

Geraint fights Sir Edyrn

Sir Edyrn rode into the field and cried out, 'My lady is the most beautiful lady in this country. If anyone says that this is not so, he must fight me. Does anyone say that his lady is more beautiful?'

Then Geraint cried out, 'There is a lady here who is far more beautiful. Come, Sir Edyrn,

and with my sword I'll make you say that Lady
Enid is more beautiful than them all.'

So they rode at each other. Geraint's spear
went through Sir Edyrn's shield, and he fell
from his horse.

Geraint got down off his horse and took his
sword. Then Sir Edyrn got up and stood ready
to fight him.

Seeing this, Enid's father came near and cried
out, 'Remember what his dwarf did to Queen
Guinevere's woman and to you.'

These words made Geraint very angry, and
he brought his sword down so hard on Sir
Edyrn's head that it cut through his helmet. He
fell. 'Do not kill me!' he cried.

'If I don't kill you,' said Geraint, 'you must
go to Queen Guinevere and ask her to forgive*
you. Your dwarf hit her woman. You saw him
do it, and you didn't stop him. If the Queen
isn't angry—if she forgives you—you shall
live.'

Sir Edyrn asks Queen Guinevere to forgive him

When King Arthur came back from riding in
the forest, the Queen told him about the knight
and the dwarf. 'And Geraint has gone to find
that knight, and fight him,' she said.

On the next evening a knight rode up to

King Arthur's castle, and a man came to tell the
King. 'He is wounded,' the man said. 'His
shield is broken, and his helmet is cut in two.
He can just sit on his horse. I have never seen
any knight so badly wounded but still alive.'

The King and Queen went out to see the
knight. It was Sir Edyrn. When he saw the
Queen, he fell at her feet and said, 'O Queen,
Sir Geraint has sent me. I ask you to forgive
me.'

Then Sir Edyrn told the King about the fight
and how strong Geraint was.

'I forgive you,' said Queen Guinevere. Then
she called some men and they took him into
the castle.

Geraint and Enid come to Camelot

On the morning after the joust, Geraint went to
the old knight and said, 'I must go back to
Camelot today. I want to take Enid with me.'

'But Enid has no beautiful clothes,' said her
father. 'The Queen mustn't see her dressed like
a poor woman.'

'She shall come dressed as she is,' said Geraint.
'Even in those poor clothes she is more beautiful
than any other lady.'

So Geraint and Enid rode to Camelot, and
they were very happy. It was evening when

they saw King Arthur's castle. Queen Guinevere looked out of the window and saw them coming. She called all her ladies: 'Come!' she said. 'We will go out to Geraint and Enid and bring them in.'

When Geraint came into the castle, the Queen said, 'Thank you, Sir Geraint, for what you have done.' Then she took Enid's hand and led her to her room and gave her one of her own dresses, and brought her into the hall; and everybody said, 'She is the most beautiful lady we have ever seen.'

So Geraint and Enid were married; and the old knight, her father, got back all that he had lost, and his brother's son was sent away out of the country.

Chapter 7
Sir Meligrance

Sir Meligrance takes the Queen away to his castle

It was the month of May, and the fields were full of flowers. The Queen called her ten knights and said, 'We will go into the fields and get flowers, and my ladies shall come with me.'

So they all rode out into the fields. When

evening came, the Queen said, 'Now we'll go back to Camelot, to King Arthur.'

As they all made ready to go, twenty men in armour came out from the forest. Then their leader cried out, 'Stand where you are—or you will be killed.'

It was Sir Meligrance. He loved Queen Guinevere and wanted to take her away to his castle.

The Queen said, 'King Arthur made you a knight: how can you do this thing to his Queen?'

The ten knights said, 'We have no armour, but we'll fight against your men who have armour. We will not see our Queen taken away without a fight.'

The ten knights could not stand against men in armour. They were all wounded, and they would have been killed; but the Queen cried out, 'I can't see my knights killed before my eyes. Don't fight any more, but come with me to Sir Meligrance's castle.'

So they all rode to the castle; but, as they went, the Queen called to her side a boy who had a very good horse. She said, 'Take this ring. Ride and take this ring to Sir Lancelot and tell him to come and save me.'

Sir Meligrance saw the boy ride away. He told his men to catch him; but they could not.

Sir Lancelot comes to save the Queen

Sir Lancelot got on his horse and rode to the castle of Sir Meligrance. When he came near the castle he thought, 'Sir Meligrance will hide his men near the road, and they will come out at me as I ride by. So I will not go along the road, but will ride through the forest.'

It was as Lancelot had thought. Sir Meligrance hid men by the road; but Sir Lancelot did not come that way.

Sir Meligrance saw Lancelot coming to the castle: all his own men were far away, waiting by the road. Then he was afraid. He went to Queen Guinevere and said, 'O Queen, forgive me for what I did. Forgive me this time. I will bring you back to Camelot and I will fight for King Arthur as a good knight.'

The Queen did not know that he had seen Lancelot and that he said this because he was afraid. So she answered, 'I forgive you.'

When Lancelot came into the castle the Queen said, 'I have forgiven Sir Meligrance. Stay here tonight. We'll go back to Camelot in the morning.'

Sir Meligrance catches Sir Lancelot

Sir Meligrance knew that Lancelot was still angry. He knew that Sir Lancelot would fight him and kill him as soon as the Queen had gone.

They sat down to eat in the great hall of the castle. When they had eaten, Sir Meligrance said to Lancelot, 'I'll lead you to your room.'

Then he led Lancelot into a room where there was a door in the floor. Sir Lancelot put his foot on the door, and it opened and he fell into a little room far down, from which he could not get out. Then Sir Meligrance went and said to the Queen, 'Sir Lancelot didn't want to stay here. He has gone back to Camelot.'

The Queen went back to Camelot, and King Arthur said, 'What is this thing that your knights tell me? They say that Sir Meligrance took you away to his castle?' And he said to Sir Meligrance, 'What is this thing that the Queen's knights are saying?'

Sir Meligrance answered, 'I didn't take the Queen away. She came with me because she loved me.'

Then the King was very angry.

Sir Lancelot fights Sir Meligrance and kills him

There was a girl in Sir Meligrance's castle. She carried food to Sir Lancelot every day. She saw how strong and brave he was. When Sir Meligrance had gone to Camelot she opened the door and Sir Lancelot went out and rode back to Camelot.

The King was sitting with the Queen and his
knights in the hall when Sir Lancelot came in.
He went up to Sir Meligrance and said, 'You
took away Queen Guinevere to your castle.
For that she forgave you; so I can't kill you for
that. Then you said that she came with you
because she loved you. For saying that I shall
kill you. I am the strongest of all King Arthur's
knights; so I'll fight without armour against
you in your armour. Even so, I shall kill you.'

So it was. Sir Meligrance came at Sir
Lancelot with his sword and struck down at his
head because he had no helmet. But Lancelot
jumped to one side, and with his sword cut Sir
Meligrance's helmet in two. And Sir Meligrance
fell dead.

Chapter 8
The Grail

Sir Galahad comes to the Seat Perilous

One day an old man dressed all in white with
a white beard came to King Arthur and said,
'O King, I have brought a young knight to you.
He is the son of a great man and he will do
great things.'

The King looked and saw a young man standing there in red armour; and his face was very beautiful.

You have read (in Chapter 1) about the Seat Perilous: it was a place at the Round Table where no knight could sit if he had ever done any bad thing to anyone. If any bad man sat in that place, he would die. Each knight had his name written on the table in his place; but in the Seat Perilous there was no name.

The old man led the young man to the Round Table, to the Seat Perilous. There was a name there—where there was no name before. It was written in gold: SIR GALAHAD.

'Sit here,' said the old man. Then he went out from the hall and was never seen again.

'Who is this young man who has sat down in the Seat Perilous and is not afraid?' the King asked. 'Does anyone know him?'

'I know him,' said Sir Lancelot. 'As I rode towards Camelot I came to a House of Good Women, and the good women brought out this young man to me saying, "His name is Galahad. You must make him a knight."'

Then many of the other knights looked at Galahad, and they saw that his face was like the face of Sir Lancelot. They remembered that, when Sir Lancelot was very young, he was married. They thought, 'That's Sir Lancelot's son.' But Sir Lancelot did not speak to the young man as a son.

The Knights of the Round Table see the Grail

As the knights sat there at the Round Table they heard a great noise. Then there was a great white light. They looked up and saw the Grail covered with a red cloth. . . . And then it had gone!

For a time no one spoke. Then Sir Galahad said, 'That is the Grail. Jesus drank from it on the night before He died. Now I know that the Grail is in this country, and I will go out and look for it. I will not come back without finding it.'

Three other knights said this same thing: they were Sir Lancelot, Sir Bors and Sir Percivale.

King Arthur was very sad. He said, 'We were all brothers, but now our Round Table is broken. You will go, and I shall not see you again.'

So the four knights rode away. For many years they looked for the Grail and did not find it.

Many other knights rode away looking for the Grail, and did not find it; and some never came back. The Round Table was not as it was; in the evening, when the King and Queen sat there, there were many unfilled places. And King Arthur was very sad.

Sir Galahad finds the Grail

After many years Sir Galahad and Sir Percivale and Sir Bors came to a place near the sea. They looked down from a hill and saw a ship. It was evening, but the ship was full of light—white light, like the light of the sun; and they knew that the Finding of the Grail was near.

They went down to the sea; and then they went into the ship. There, on a table, Galahad saw the Grail.

Then a great sleep came on them. The ship went out to sea. When they opened their eyes they saw that they had come to a city.

Sir Galahad said, 'We must take the table and the Grail out of the ship.'

So they took the table and the Grail into the city.

Sir Galahad becomes King, and how he dies

The king of that country was very ill. He died; and the people did not know whom to have as king after him. The great men were sitting in the city-hall to find a new king. Then an old man came into the hall—an old man dressed all in white with a white beard. He said, 'Take as your king the youngest of these three knights who have come to your city. He shall be your king.' Then he went out from the hall, and no one saw him come, or saw him go.

So Galahad was made king.

Sir Bors went back to Camelot. Sir Percivale lived alone, giving himself to God.

Sir Galahad did not live long. He said, 'I have seen the Grail, and I am happy. I do not want to live long.'

He built a beautiful church and put the Grail in it.

Soon after that the same old man came to him and said, 'Your work is done. God calls you.'

In the morning they found him in front of the Grail, dead; and his face was very happy.

Chapter 9
King Arthur dies

Mordred makes himself King in Arthur's place

King Arthur was angry with Lancelot. Lancelot went over the sea to France, and King Arthur and Sir Gawain went there to fight him.

While Arthur was out of England, an evil knight named Sir Mordred came to Camelot and said to Queen Guinevere, 'King Arthur has gone out of the country and he is dead. I am now king, and you must be my queen.'

Then Guinevere ran away to The Tower of London; and all her men went with her. Mordred came, but the walls were very strong, and he could not break in.

King Arthur comes back from France

Soon Mordred heard that King Arthur was coming back to England with many ships and with all his men. So Mordred went with all his men, and there was a great fight. Sir Mordred's men could not stand against King Arthur: they ran from the field. But Sir Gawain was wounded. He said to King Arthur, 'I am dying. Give me a pen and paper so that I may write to Sir Lancelot.' He wrote:

> To Lancelot, bravest of all knights.
> Today I was wounded in the fight, and I
> know that I am dying. Because of the love
> that we had for each other, come quickly
> and help King Arthur.

He asked Arthur to send this quickly to Lancelot; and then he died.

Arthur sees Gawain in his sleep

Sir Mordred got more men and came to a place near the Lake where Arthur had gone with Merlin to get Excalibur; and there King Arthur came against him.

On the night before the fight, Arthur saw Gawain in his sleep. Gawain said, 'Don't fight Mordred now. After one month Lancelot will come with all his men and help you, and save the Queen.'

When the King awoke, day had come. He called his knights and said, 'There will be no fighting today. I shall go and speak with Mordred. Come with me. Bring your swords, but they must stay in their scabbards. . . . If Mordred or any of his knights puts his hand to his sword, then fight and kill!'

King Arthur kills Mordred

A man came and told Mordred, 'King Arthur is coming to speak with you. Tell your knights this, "Your swords must stay in their scabbards. If any man puts his hand to his sword, then the King and his knights will fight and kill."'

King Arthur stood speaking with Mordred. All King Arthur's knights stood near him; and Mordred's knights stood near Mordred.

As they stood there, a snake★ came out of the

grass and bit a knight on his foot, and he took
his sword to kill it. Then, seeing one knight put
his hand to his sword, all the knights began to
fight.

They fought all day. When evening came,
the King saw that two of his knights, Sir
Lucan and Sir Bedivere, were alive. Sir Lucan
was badly wounded. All the others were dead,
and Mordred stood with his sword alone: all
his men had been killed.

Then the King ran at Mordred with a spear,
and the spear went through his body; but, as
Mordred fell, he wounded King Arthur with
his sword.

*Sir Lucan and Sir Bedivere take the dying King
from the field*

Sir Lucan and Sir Bedivere took the King to a
little church which stood near the field. But,
as they came there and set the King down, Sir
Lucan fell and died of his wound. And Sir
Bedivere was alone.

Then King Arthur said, 'I must soon die too.
So take my sword Excalibur, and go to the lake
and throw it into the water.'

Sir Bedivere said, 'I will do it.' So he took
the sword, but, as he walked to the lake he saw
the jewels on it, and he thought, 'If I throw

this beautiful sword into the lake, what good will that do?' So he hid Excalibur by a big stone, and went back to the King, and said, 'I have done what you told me to do. I have thrown your sword into the lake.'

'What did you see there?' the King asked.

'I saw the water, and the sky, and the stones. That is all.'

'You didn't do as I told you,' King Arthur said. 'Go again, and throw Excalibur into the water, and come back and tell me what you saw.'

Sir Bedivere throws Excalibur into the lake

Sir Bedivere went again to the lake and took the sword from its hiding place. But as he looked at it and saw how beautiful it was, he thought, 'I can't throw this sword into the water. It shall be at my side so long as I live, and I shall remember King Arthur.' So he hid it again, and went back to King Arthur, and said, 'I have thrown Excalibur into the lake. I saw the water, and the stones and the sky, and I saw the sword fall into the lake.'

'Go again,' the King said very sadly. 'If you don't do it this time, I'll kill you with my hands.'

So Sir Bedivere went again. He took the

sword from its hiding place. Then he threw it far over the water. An arm came up out of the water and caught the sword, then took it down into the lake.

Sir Bedivere went back and told the King what he had seen.

'Now,' said King Arthur, 'take me to the lake.'

So Sir Bedivere took the King down to the lake; and, when he came there, he saw a black ship at the side of the water. In it there were many ladies, all dressed in black.

As he looked at their faces, he thought, 'These are the faces of many women whom I have known, women who have died but who are still remembered.'

King Arthur said, 'Please put me on the ship.'

So Sir Bedivere set him down in the ship; and the ladies stood round him.

The ship went out over the water, and Sir Bedivere stood there alone.

Questions

Chapter 1 Arthur and Merlin

1 Where did King Arthur live? 2 Who did King Uther want to marry? 3 What was Merlin? 4 What did the knights begin to do? 5 Where were all the great men to go? — To — 6 What was in the stone? 7 Where did Sir Ector and the two young men go? 8 How did Arthur get a sword? 9 What did Merlin make? 10 The Seat Perilous was for a man who had — — — —. What?

Chapter 2 The Sword Excalibur

1 What did Arthur see from the forest? 2 Who told Sir Pellinore to fight? 3 What did Arthur's sword do? 4 What did Arthur see in the lake? 5 What did he do with Excalibur? 6 What did Sir Damas ask King Arthur to do? 7 Why was Arthur unhappy? 8 What did Morgan le Fay take? 9 What did Arthur see from the top of the hill? 10 Where did Morgan le Fay go?

Chapter 3 Vivien and Merlin

1 'Can't you save yourself?' What was the answer? 2 Who did Vivien learn magic from? (2 people) 3 What did she want to be? 4 What does Merlin NOT know? 5 What did Vivien do to Merlin?

Chapter 4 Sir Tristram

1 Where did the Queen of Lyonesse have her son? 2 Who drank the poison? 3 Who was Sir Marhaus? 4 Sir Tristram's wound did not heal. Why? — Because... 5 Where did the poison come from? 6 Who healed Tristram's wound? 7 What armour did Sir Palamides have? 8 Who did King Mark want to marry? 9 Who went to Ireland to bring Isolt to Cornwall? 10 Who killed King Mark?

Chapter 5 Gareth and Linet

1 What did the young man want? — To eat ... 2 What did Linet call Gareth? — A — — 3 Where did Linet ride? 4 Where did Gareth and Noon fight? 5 What did Gareth take from Noon? 6 What did Linet call out? 7 Where did Gareth throw Evening? 8 Where did Gareth and Linet eat? 9 What was on Night's shield? 10 What did Gareth see when he opened Night's helmet?

Chapter 6 Geraint and Enid

1 Geraint had no — but he had a —. 2 Where will the Queen wait? 3 What three people did they see? 1 ——; 2 ——; 3 ——. 4 Why did not Geraint fight? 'Because he had no —.' 5 Who opened the castle door? 6 Who took Geraint's horse? 7 What did the old knight bring to Geraint? 8 What did Geraint remember? 9 Who came to King Arthur's castle? 10 What did Guinevere give to Enid?

Chapter 7 Sir Meligrance

1 Who went with the Queen? 'Her — — and her —.' 2 Who came out from the forest? 3 Who took the Queen's ring to Sir Lancelot? 4 Where did Sir Meligrance hide his men? 5 Where did Lancelot ride? 6 What did the Queen say when Lancelot came? 'I have — — —.' 7 Where did Lancelot fall? 'Through — —.' 8 What did Meligrance say? 'The Queen came with me because — — — —.' 9 Who opened the door of Lancelot's room? 10 How did Lancelot fight Meligrance?

Chapter 8 The Grail

1 Who brought Sir Galahad? 2 Where did Sir Galahad sit? 3 The other Knights thought, 'Sir Galahad is ———'s son.' 4 What covered the Grail? 5 Which four knights went to look for the Grail? 6 What did Sir Galahad see from the hill? 7 What was on the table? 8 What did they see when they woke? 9 Where did Sir Galahad put the Grail? 10 What did the old man say to Sir Galahad?

Chapter 9 King Arthur dies

1 Where were Arthur and Gawain? 2 Who came to Camelot? 3 Where did Guinevere go? 4 Who was wounded and dying? 5 Why did a knight take out his sword? 6 How many of Arthur's knights were alive in the evening? 7 Where did the two knights take King Arthur? 8 What did Arthur tell Bedivere to do? 9 What did Bedivere do with Excalibur? 10 Where did Bedivere put King Arthur?

List of extra words

chapter		chapter		chapter	
1	archbishop, armour	4	harp, heal	4	slower
2	break, broke, broken	1	helmet	9	snake
2	castle	1	joust	1	spear
6	dwarf	1	knight	4	strong
2	evil	2	lake	4	wound
6	forgive	4	poison		
8	Grail	1	scabbard, shield		